Ta

Th
a f

Once upon a time there lived a poor boy called Dick Whittington. He was a happy lad. He was also brave and adventurous.

One day he heard folks in the village saying the streets of London were paved with gold.

"Hmm!" he thought. "I must go and seek my fortune there." So he tied bread and cheese in a cloth and set off.

Dick walked for miles. When he arrived
he found the streets were full of stones
and bones, and all kinds of rubbish.
There was not a scrap of gold
anywhere to be seen!

Dick's tummy rumbled with hunger.
His feet were sore. He was so tired he
curled up in a doorway and fell asleep.

Next morning, a kind merchant called Mr Fitzwarren and his daughter, Alice, found Dick on their doorstep. "Oh, you poor lad," said the merchant. "You must come inside and have some food."

Mr Fitzwarren offered Dick a job in the
kitchens. Dick was very grateful.

But the cook was a mean woman.

She scolded Dick and beat him.

At night, rats scuttled around his
bedroom. They even ran over his bed.
So Dick bought a cat. He grew very fond
of her, and so did Alice.

One day, there was hustle and bustle everywhere. Mr Fitzwarren was loading his ship with goods to sell in far off lands.

"If you wish me to sell your things for you I will," he told his servants. "You might make a fortune."

Dick knew he needed money, but all he had to sell was his lovely cat. His heart sank as he handed her over to the merchant.

Alice put her arm round him.

"I'm sure she will be all right," she said.

Alice became a good friend to Dick.

But the cook did not become Dick's

friend. In fact, she beat Dick even harder.

One day Dick could stand it no
longer. He ran away.

He walked to the edge of town and sat down on a hillside. He felt really sad, and he missed Alice. The church bells from the town began to ring.

"Turn again Whittington," they seemed to say. "Turn again Whittington, Lord Mayor of London."

"Those bells are telling me to go back," thought Dick. "I must go."

He hurried all the way to the merchant's house, and to Alice.

There was hustle and bustle everywhere. Mr Fitzwarren was home! He had brought back gold and wealth for himself and his servants. He handed Dick a big bag of gold.

Dick was amazed. All he could say was, "Oh Sir! Oh thank you, Sir!" The merchant smiled. "You're welcome, Dick. The King of Barbary bought your cat. He wanted it to kill all the rats in his palace."

"You deserve it Dick," said Alice.

She gave him a big kiss.

"And there's more good news.

The horrid cook has gone!"

When he was older, Dick married Alice.
He did become Lord Mayor of London.
And both times the bells rang louder
than ever through London Town.
"Dick Whittington," they said.
"Lord Mayor of London."

About the story

Dick Whittington is an English folk tale that was first written down in 1605. The main character is based on a real person, Richard Whittington, who was Lord Mayor of London between 1397 and 1420. The real Richard Whittington's wife was called Alice Fitzwarren. But Richard Whittington was never poor. He came from a wealthy family. It is not even certain that he owned a cat! He is remembered for his many good deeds towards the poor people of London.

Be in the story!

Imagine you are Dick. How do you feel after you leave Mr Fitzwarren's house?

Now imagine you are Alice. How do you feel when Dick comes home and makes his fortune?